BIBLE STUDY
MADE EASY

HENDRICKSON PUBLISHERS · ROSE PUBLISHING

Bible Study Made Easy
©2018 Rose Publishing, LLC

Rose Publishing, LLC
P.O. Box 3473
Peabody, Massachusetts 01961-3473 USA
www.hendricksonrose.com

Cover and layout design by Cristalle Kishi.

Photos provided by Shutterstock.com.

Printed in the United States of America
010718VP

CONTENTS

———

How to Begin 5

   Basic Tips for Bible Study..............................6

   Seven Ways to Read the Bible.......................8

   Become Familiar with the Bible...................10

   How to Choose a Bible Version....................14

What Is the Bible?..**22**

   Ten Things to Know about the Bible......... 22

   All the Books of the Bible............................ 26

Four Steps of Inductive Bible Study...............**36**

   The "SOIL" Approach................................... 37

   Step 1: Selection 39

   Step 2: Observation 45

   Step 3: Interpretation 50

   Step 4: Life Application 54

The Bible Study Toolbox **58**

   Study Bibles... 58

   Concordances.. 60

   Bible Software and Websites 61

   Bible Dictionaries...62

Bible Atlases, Maps, and Time Lines 63

Bible Commentaries and Handbooks 64

Specialty Bibles 65

Building a Bible Reference Library 66

How to Tackle the Tough Parts **67**

The Five "Do Nots" of Interpretation 68

Understanding Figurative Language 71

Discovering the Intended Meaning 73

Bible Background **74**

Reading the Old Testament 74

Reading the New Testament 78

Let's Try It! A Sample Bible Study **87**

The Goal of Bible Study **92**

Seven Reasons to Study the Bible 93

HOW TO BEGIN

GOD'S WORD can change your heart and transform your life. The Bible wasn't written to be merely history or a piece of great literature. It is meant to be read with both the mind and heart. God loves you and wants you to love him. As Deuteronomy 8:3 reminds us, "Man does not live on bread alone but on every word that comes from the mouth of the Lord."

Studying the Bible does not mean becoming an expert in one passage or book. It means we dig deeply so we can be deeply transformed. The more we know about God, the more we can love him.

God gave the Bible to the church. Reading and studying the Bible in community is very rewarding. Share what you've learned with others. Their questions will challenge you to pray and study more to find the answers.

"Read it through; pray it in;
live it out; pass it on."
—GEORGE GRITTER

Basic Tips for Bible Study

✢ Plan a Study Time

Decide on a quiet time and place to study God's Word and make it a daily habit, like eating. Some people get up early to spend time with God. Others study during the day or evening.

✢ Pray

Ask God to help you understand his Word. Pray using your own words or something like this: "Lord, thank you for the Bible, which teaches us who you are and what you want for our lives. Please help me understand it and do what you want me to do." In Jeremiah 33:3, God promises: "Call to me and I will answer you and tell you great and unsearchable things you do not know."

✢ Read and Re-read It

The Bible is the most important letter you can ever receive—a message from the God of the universe who made you, loves you, and wants to communicate with you. Open your "love letter" every day. Re-read each chapter and verse several times.

✢ Know the Author

Read Genesis to learn about the God who created the world. All Scripture is inspired by God. God actually visited Earth in the form of man—the man Christ Jesus. Jesus said, "I and the Father are one" (John 10:30). Read the Gospel of John to learn about God's plan for you.

✢ Take Notes

Write notes about what you read. Use a specific notebook or journal especially for Bible study. The four steps of inductive Bible study will help you look at God's word and discover how it applies to you. You might want to underline key verses or write notes in the margin of your Bible.

✢ Make the Bible Your Authority

Accept and believe that what the Bible says is true. You may not understand everything in the Bible, but obey and apply what you do understand.

Seven Ways to Read the Bible

1 **Prayerfully**

Before you begin, ask God to speak. Ask him for "ears to hear."

2 **Expectantly**

Believe that God wants to speak to you, even more than you want to hear from him. Then be alert for his voice.

3 **Devotionally**

See your Bible reading as personal time with God rather than an assignment to learn new information about God.

4 **Slowly**

Don't be in a rush. Linger. Savor the words.

5 **Comprehensively**

Read through a whole book of the Bible. Don't ignore big sections of Scripture. Consider reading the entire Bible cover to cover. That's the best way to get the truest sense of who God is, and what his story is about.

6 **Regularly**

Exercising once every three weeks is better than nothing, but it isn't likely to get you in great physical condition. In the same way, occasional Bible reading isn't the optimal way to cultivate your relationship with God or prepare for helping others know God.

7 **Obediently**

Always read with a mind-set of "I will do whatever God commands."

Become Familiar with the Bible

✛ Memorize the order of the books of the Bible.

THE OLD TESTAMENT

PENTATEUCH	POETRY & WISDOM	PROPHETIC	
Genesis	Job	**MAJOR**	
Exodus	Psalms	Isaiah	
Leviticus	Proverbs	Jeremiah	
Numbers	Ecclesiastes	Lamentations	
Deuteronomy	Song of Songs (Song of Solomon)	Ezekiel	
		Daniel	
HISTORICAL		**MINOR**	
Joshua		Hosea	
Judges		Joel	
Ruth		Amos	
1 Samuel		Obadiah	
2 Samuel		Jonah	
1 Kings		Micah	
2 Kings		Nahum	
1 Chronicles		Habakkuk	
2 Chronicles		Zephaniah	
Ezra		Haggai	
Nehemiah		Zechariah	
Esther		Malachi	

NEW TESTAMENT

GOSPELS	PAULINE EPISTLES	GENERAL EPISTLES
Matthew	Romans	Hebrews
Mark	1 Corinthians	James
Luke	2 Corinthians	1 Peter
John	Galatians	2 Peter
	Ephesians	1 John
Acts (of the Apostles)	Philippians	2 John
	Colossians	3 John
	1 Thessalonians	Jude
	2 Thessalonians	Revelation
	1 Timothy	
	2 Timothy	
	Titus	
	Philemon	

✢ Learn how to read Bible references.

For example: Psalm 23:2
Psalm = Name of letter or book
23: = chapter
:2 = verse

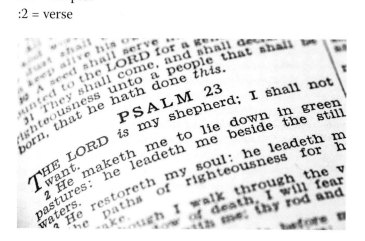

✢ Know the type of book you're reading.

Is it a book about history, poetry or wisdom literature, a book by a prophet, one of the four Gospels, the book of Acts, or an epistle (letter)?

✢ Reflect on Scripture daily.

Reflection (also called meditation) means that we allow the Bible to settle in our minds and hearts. We do this by thinking about it all day long, wondering what a passage or a verse means for us throughout the day's activities.

Write a verse or passage on a small piece of paper and carry it along with you. If you are standing in line, waiting at a restaurant, or have another free moment, take the paper out and think about how the text connects to your life at that specific time.

✣ Memorize Bible verses.

When scuba divers face problems underwater, they rely on their previous training to find a way out. When we face temptation or sudden grief, our "training" will kick in. All those Bible verses we have memorized will come back. God will speak to us through them in unexpected ways.

One of the best ways to memorize something is by finding partners who help and challenge you to work together.

How to Choose a Bible Version

There are many different Bible translations to choose from. Find a version that is most helpful for the type of Bible study you will be doing.

There are three main methods of Bible translation:

- Word-for-Word
- Balance
- Thought-for-Thought

There is also paraphrasing, which is slightly different than translation.

✢ Word-for-Word

Scholars attempt to translate each word based upon the word usage at the time of the writing. This is the strictest translation method. No translation is actually word-for-word, but the intent of this method is to come as close as possible.

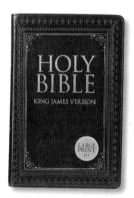

Examples:

- King James Version (KJV)
- New American Standard Bible (NASB)
- Revised Standard Version (RSV)

✣ Balance

A middle balance between a word-for-word and thought-for-thought approach. This is a happy medium, intended to create a translation that is close to the original and also readable.

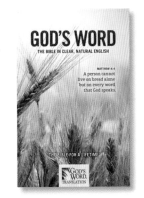

Examples:

- New International Version (NIV)
- God's Word Translation (GW)

✣ Thought-for-Thought (also known as "Dynamic Equivalence")

Scholars translate the meaning of each thought. This is a looser translation method, which is great for ease of reading.

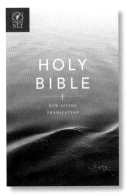

Examples:

- Good News Translation (GNT)
- New Living Translation (NLT)
- New Century Version (NCV)

⁜ Paraphrase

This is a restatement of a translation in modern terms and vocabulary, often expanded (or "amplified") for clarity. This method is not intended to be a direct translation, but is easy for modern-day readers to understand and connect with.

Example:

- The Message (MSG)

Take a look at the chart on the next page to see a well-known passage handled all four ways. Each method is valuable, and as you can see, they often have more in common than not. Choose the one that best fits your needs.

TRANSLATION METHOD	JOHN 3:16–17
WORD-FOR-WORD (NASB)	For God so loved the world, that He gave His only begotten Son, that whoever believes in Him shall not perish, but have eternal life. For God did not send the Son into the world to judge the world, but that the world might be saved through Him.
BALANCE (NIV)	For God so loved the world that he gave his one and only Son, that whoever believes in him shall not perish but have eternal life. For God did not send his Son into the world to condemn the world, but to save the world through him.
THOUGHT-FOR-THOUGHT (NLT)	For this is how God loved the world: He gave his one and only Son, so that everyone who believes in him will not perish but have eternal life. God sent his Son into the world not to judge the world, but to save the world through him.
PARAPHRASE (MSG)	This is how much God loved the world: He gave his Son, his one and only Son. And this is why: so that no one need be destroyed; by believing in him, anyone can have a whole and lasting life. God didn't go to all the trouble of sending his Son merely to point an accusing finger, telling the world how bad it was. He came to help, to put the world right again.

OVERVIEW OF POPULAR ENGLISH BIBLE VERSIONS

TRANSLATION	YEAR*	TYPE
King James Version (KJV)	1611, 1769	Word-for-word
American Standard Version (ASV)	1901	Word-for-word
Revised Standard Version (RSV)	1952, 1971	Word-for-word
Amplified Bible (AMP)	1965, 2015	Word-for-word, plus amplification of meaning
New Jerusalem Bible (NJB)	1966, 1985	Word-for-word
New American Bible (NAB)	1970, 1986, 1991	Word-for-word
New American Standard Bible (NASB)	1971, 1995	Word-for-word
Good News Translation (GNT)	1976, 1992	Thought-for-thought
New International Version (NIV)	1978, 1984, 2011	Balance
New King James Version (NKJV)	1982	Word-for-word
New Century Version (NCV)	1987, 1991	Thought-for-thought

DESCRIPTION

Used by adults who prefer the English found in older versions.

Very formal. Used for serious Bible study.

Based on the ASV

Uses a unique system of punctuation, typefaces, and synonyms (in parentheses) to more fully explain words.

Typically used by Roman Catholics for serious Bible study. Includes the Apocrypha.

Official translation used in U.S. Catholic Church Mass. Includes the Apocrypha.

Used by adults for serious Bible study.

Used by children and believers for whom English is not their first language.

Modern translation aimed to be acceptable to many denominations. Currently the best-selling Bible version.

Modern language translation to maintain the structure and beauty of the KJV.

Uses footnotes to clarify ancient customs. Used by children, teenagers, and adults for personal devotional reading.

TRANSLATION	YEAR*	TYPE
New Revised Standard Version (NRSV)	1989	Word-for-word
Contemporary English Version (CEV)	1995	Thought-for-thought
God's Word Translation (GW)	1995	Balance
New International Reader's Version (NIrV)	1996, 1998, 2014	Thought-for-thought
New Living Translation (NLT)	1996, 2004, 2007, 2013, 2015	Thought-for-thought
English Standard Version (ESV)	2001	Word-for-word
The Message (MSG)	2002	Paraphrase
Christian Standard Bible (CSB)	2004, 2017	Balance
Common English Bible (CEB)	2011	Balance

DESCRIPTION

Revision of the RSV using information gathered from newly discovered Hebrew and Greek manuscripts.

Recommended for children and people who do not speak English as their first language.

Translated by a committee of biblical scholars and English reviewers to ensure accurate, natural English.

Simple words and short sentences to appeal to a lower reading level.

Easy-to-read modern version.

Derived from the RSV. Used by teenagers and adults for serious Bible study.

Re-creates the common language in which the Bible was written into today's common language.

Used by teenagers and adults for personal devotions and Bible study. Revision of the Holman Christian Standard Bible (HCSB).

Diverse team of translators from 22 faith traditions in American, African, Asian, European, and Latino communities.

*Year complete Bible translation was released and later revisions

WHAT IS THE BIBLE?

Ten Things to Know about the Bible

THE BIBLE is the most printed and read book in history. More evidence exists to confirm the Bible than to confirm any other ancient historical documents.

1 The Bible is inspired by God. As 2 Timothy 3:16–17 states: "All Scripture is God-breathed and is useful for teaching, rebuking, correcting and training in righteousness, so that the servant of God may be thoroughly equipped for every good work" (see also 2 Peter 1:20–21).

2 The Bible is made up of 66 different books.

- They were written over 1,600 years (from approximately 1500 BC to AD 100) by more than 40 kings, prophets, leaders, and followers of Jesus.

- The Old Testament has 39 books (written approximately 1500–400 BC).

- The New Testament has 27 books (written approximately AD 45–100).

- The Hebrew Bible has the same text as the English Bible's Old Testament, but divides and arranges it differently.

3 The Old Testament was written mainly in Hebrew, with some Aramaic. The New Testament was written in Greek.

4 The books of the Bible were collected and arranged and recognized as inspired sacred authority by councils of rabbis and councils of church leaders based on careful guidelines.

5 Before the printing press was invented, the Bible was copied by hand. The Bible was copied very accurately, in many cases by special scribes who developed intricate methods of counting words and letters to ensure that no errors had been made.

6 The Bible was the first book ever printed on the printing press with movable type (Gutenberg Press, 1455, Latin Bible).

7 There is much evidence that the Bible we have today is remarkably true to the original writings. Of the thousands of copies made by hand before 1500, nearly 5,900 Greek manuscripts from the New Testament alone still exist today. The text of the Bible is better preserved than the writings of Plato or Aristotle.

8 The discovery of the Dead Sea Scrolls confirmed the astonishing reliability of some of the copies of the Old Testament made over the years. Although some spelling variations exist, no variation affects basic Bible doctrines.

The Qumran caves, where the Dead Sea Scrolls were discovered.

9 As the Bible was carried to other countries, it was translated into the common language of the people by scholars who wanted others to know God's Word. Today there are still about 2,000 groups with no Bible in their own language.

■ By AD 200, the Bible was translated into seven languages;

■ By 500, 13 languages;

■ By 900, 17 languages;

■ By 1400, 28 languages;

■ By 1800, 57 languages;

■ By 1900, 537 languages;

■ By 1980, 1,100 languages;

■ By 2014, 2,883 languages had some portions of Scripture.

(Source: The Wycliffe Global Alliance)

(Excerpt from *How We Got the Bible*, Rose Publishing.)

All the Books of the Bible

The 66 books of the Bible are divided into two main sections: the Old Testament and the New Testament.

✛ The Old Testament

The Old Testament reveals God's loving plan of salvation, from Creation to prophecies of the future Messiah (the Savior).

There are four parts of the Old Testament:

- Pentateuch (or Law)
- Historical Books
- Poetry and Wisdom Books
- Prophetic Books: Major Prophets and Minor Prophets

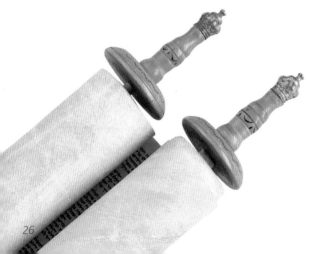

PENTATEUCH (LAW)

The Pentateuch contains stories about the creation of the world, the flood, Abraham, Isaac, Jacob, the children of Israel in Egypt, the exodus, and the time the children of Israel spent in the wilderness before entering the Promised Land.

The books also record the law God gave to the people on Mount Sinai, which laid down the regulations for sacrifice, worship, and daily living. The Pentateuch is also called the Torah.

Books of the Pentateuch

GENESIS	The beginnings of creation, the nations, and the Israelites
EXODUS	God's deliverance of the Israelites from slavery in Egypt
LEVITICUS	Law and sacrifice
NUMBERS	Census and history of the Israelites in the wilderness
DEUTERONOMY	Moses' final sermons

HISTORICAL BOOKS

The Historical Books continue with the story of the people of Israel and the conquest of the Promised Land in the book of Joshua, the continuous cycle of disobedience in the book of Judges, the first kings and the united and divided kingdoms, the Assyrian invasion, Babylonian invasion, the years in exile, and the return from exile during the Persian rule.

Historical Books	
JOSHUA	History of the conquest of the Promised Land
JUDGES	Cycles of sin and deliverance in the Promised Land
RUTH	A story of a faithful foreigner
1 & 2 SAMUEL	God is king, but we want an earthly king
1 & 2 KINGS	The limits of human rule
1 & 2 CHRONICLES	Still the people of God
EZRA	History of the first and second waves of Jews who returned to Jerusalem
NEHEMIAH	History of the third wave of Jews who returned to Jerusalem
ESTHER	A story of courage in dangerous times

POETRY AND WISDOM BOOKS

The Poetry and Wisdom books include hymns, proverbs, poems, and dramas. They illustrate the creative ways the people of Israel expressed themselves to God and to each other.

These books deal with questions that affect humans everywhere and at any time: questions about human suffering, death, what makes for a good life, and knowledge for living. Poetry has a unique ability to express deep feelings and thoughts in effective and beautiful ways.

Poetry and Wisdom Books	
JOB	A story of suffering and trust
PSALMS	A collection of poetic songs
PROVERBS	Wisdom for godly living
ECCLESIASTES	Searching for meaning and truth
SONG OF SONGS (OR SONG OF SOLOMON)	A love song

PROPHETIC BOOKS: THE MAJOR AND MINOR PROPHETS

The Major Prophets are not called *major* because of their message or quality, but rather because of the length of the books. The prophets brought God's words, which included warnings of judgment, warnings and hope for the immediate future (as well as warnings and hope for the distant future), and hope in the coming Messiah.

The Major Prophets	
ISAIAH	Judgment and salvation
JEREMIAH	Judgment, wrath, and weeping
LAMENTATIONS	Dirge poem (lament)
EZEKIEL	Prophecies and visions of God's presence
DANIEL	Life in exile and visions of the future

The Minor Prophets, also called "The Book of the Twelve" in the Hebrew Bible, are just as important as the Major Prophets. They are called *minor* because of their shorter length. They also brought God's words to the people regarding judgment and hope.

The Minor Prophets

HOSEA	Warnings to a spiritually adulterous nation
JOEL	Prophecies about the great and dreadful day of the Lord
AMOS	Warnings to a society gone awry
OBADIAH	A vision against Edom
JONAH	A story of God's mercy
MICAH	A call to seek justice, love mercy, and walk humbly
NAHUM	Prophecy about the destruction of Nineveh
HABAKKUK	A prophet asks God about justice and mercy
ZEPHANIAH	Warnings about judgment on the day of the Lord
HAGGAI	A message to rebuild the temple
ZECHARIAH	Visions and messages about the Lord's reign over all
MALACHI	The coming day of the Lord

✣ The New Testament

The New Testament consists of twenty-seven books. These books reveal God's salvation of sinful humankind by the suffering, death, and resurrection of the Messiah, Jesus Christ, and reveal the everlasting kingdom of God.

THE GOSPELS AND ACTS

The four Gospels narrate the life of Jesus Christ—his birth, ministry, death, and resurrection.

The book of Acts tells the story of the first Christians.

The Gospels and Acts	
MATTHEW	Jesus, the promised Messiah
MARK	Jesus, the suffering Son of Man
LUKE	Jesus, the Savior of the world
JOHN	Jesus, the Son of God
ACTS	The story of the early church

THE EPISTLES AND REVELATION

The twenty-one epistles are letters from early church leaders to churches and believers. The epistles are traditionally grouped into two sections: the Pauline Epistles, which are the thirteen letters written by the apostle Paul, and the eight General Epistles, which are letters written by other apostles or leaders.

Paul's letters were written to young churches, pastors, and friends to guide, encourage, and correct them as they lived as followers of Jesus.

The Pauline Epistles	
ROMANS	A letter about the power of the gospel
1 CORINTHIANS	A letter to clear up misunderstandings
2 CORINTHIANS	Paul's most personal letter
GALATIANS	A letter about justification by faith
EPHESIANS	A letter about living in God-honoring ways
PHILIPPIANS	A letter about living like Christ

The Pauline Epistles (continued)

COLOSSIANS	A letter about the supremacy of Christ
1 THESSALONIANS	A letter about hope in the face of persecution
2 THESSALONIANS	A letter about being ready
1 TIMOTHY	Instructions for leading a church
2 TIMOTHY	A letter about persevering
TITUS	Instructions for church leadership and upright living
PHILEMON	An appeal for reconciliation

The General Epistles were written by a variety of early church leaders, including Peter, James, and John, to provide encouragement to Christians facing persecution and to warn them about false teachings.

The book of Revelation is unique in the New Testament because it is the only book that is written in an apocalyptic style; it relates its message through signs, symbols, dreams, and visions.

The General Epistles & Revelation

HEBREWS	A letter about the superiority of Christ
JAMES	A letter about having a living faith
1 PETER	A letter about suffering
2 PETER	A letter about trusting the prophecies and promises of God
1 JOHN	A letter about love
2 JOHN	A letter about discernment
3 JOHN	A letter about loving others vs. loving to be first
JUDE	A letter about contending for the faith
REVELATION	Visions that reveal God's glory and triumph

FOUR STEPS OF INDUCTIVE BIBLE STUDY

THERE ARE all kinds of ways to approach Bible study. One of the simplest, clearest, and easiest methods is inductive Bible study.

- Inductive reasoning moves from specific examples to general conclusions.
- Deductive reasoning moves from general examples to specific conclusions.

So *inductive* Bible study starts in specific passages in the Bible (instead of a secondary source) and uses those passages to get to broader biblical truths.

SPECIFIC
Bible Passages

GENERAL
Biblical Truths

The "SOIL" Approach

Bible study is important to our growth as followers of Jesus. In a parable, Jesus compares the word of God with a seed. The seed planted in good soil represents those with honest and good hearts, who hear the word, apply it, and with patience produce a crop or fruit.

"This is the meaning of the parable: The seed is the word of God. Those along the path are the ones who hear, and then the devil comes and takes away the word from their hearts, so that they may not believe and be saved. Those on the rocky ground are the ones who receive the word with joy when they hear it, but they have no root. They believe for a while, but in the time of testing they fall away. The seed that fell among thorns stands for those who hear, but as they go on their way they are choked by life's worries, riches and pleasures, and they do not mature. But the seed on good soil stands for those with a noble and good heart, who hear the word, retain it, and by persevering produce a crop."

—LUKE 8:11–15

An easy way to remember how to do inductive Bible study is with the acronym SOIL:

S ELECTION
What Do I Study?

O BSERVATION
What Do I See?

I NTERPRETATION
What Does It Mean?

L IFE APPLICATION
How Does It Apply?

STEP 1
SELECTION

What Do I Study?

"I delight in your decrees;
I will not neglect your word."

PSALM 119:16

Most Bibles are divided not only into books, chapters, and verses but also into sections with topical headings, so it's easy to see where a passage begins and ends. While picking a passage at random is always an option, it's not usually the best one. Here a few suggestions of where to start your study—from entire books to short passages.

✣ Starter Books

- **Genesis**, the first book of the Bible, is a great place to start. It begins with God's creation of the world and of humans in his image, and continues through his covenant with Abraham and his descendants, who become God's people, Israel.

- **The Gospel of John** tells the story of Jesus' life from a different perspective than Matthew, Mark or Luke. John's view is unique and approachable. Pair it with Mark, the shortest Gospel, if you want to see what the differences between John and the first three Gospels are all about.

⁜ Gospel Comparison

Jesus' life is a natural focal point of Bible study. Studying a whole Gospel is a great way to learn more about Jesus, but you can also study specific events in his life by comparing parallel passages in multiple Gospels.

Try picking an event from the table below and reading the relevant passages to see how each Gospel writer described it.

EVENT	MATTHEW	MARK	LUKE	JOHN
Jesus calms a storm.	8:18–27	4:35–41	8:22–25	Not recorded in John.
Jesus' triumphal entry into Jerusalem.	21:1–17	11:1–11	19:29–44	12:12–19
Peter denies knowing Jesus.	26:69–75	14:66–72	22:55–65	18:25–27

✦ Key Passages

If you'd rather start small, here are seven passages that can teach you about God and Christian life.

1 **The Fall of Humanity**—Genesis 3

2 **The Ten Commandments**—Exodus 20:1–17

3 **The Prophecy of the Coming Messiah**—Isaiah 53

4 **The Beatitudes**—Matthew 5:1–11

5 **The Sermon on the Mount**—Matthew 5–7

6 **Two Great Commandments**—Matthew 22:36–40

7 **The Prodigal Son**—Luke 15:11–32

✜ The Seven "I Ams" in the Gospel of John

In the Gospel of John, Jesus teaches the famous seven "I ams" to illustrate who he is. Studying these statements (and their contexts) is another way to explore Jesus' identity and role as our Savior.

1 "I am the bread of life" (6:35).

2 "I am the light of the world" (8:12; 9:5).

3 "I am the gate" (10:7, 9).

4 "I am the good shepherd" (10:11).

5 "I am the resurrection and the life" (11:25).

6 "I am the way and the truth and the life" (14:6).

7 "I am the true vine" (15:1).

✢ Word Studies in Paul's Writings

The apostle Paul's letters in the New Testament give us much of our information about Christian living in the early church, as well as valuable guidance for pursuing Christian life today. It's good to study an entire letter—and many of them, like Galatians, Ephesians, Philippians, and Colossians, are manageably short—but you can also study specific words and concepts that Paul discussed frequently across his letters.

For example, use a concordance to look up *faith*, *love*, *law*, or *grace* in Paul's letters and see all the ways Paul used those words.

✜ Character Studies of Old Testament Figures

While you have your concordance out, consider brushing up on your knowledge of major Old Testament figures. Study Abraham or Moses—how they lived and interacted with God in Genesis through Deuteronomy, and how they were spoken of in other Old Testament books and in the New Testament. While you're learning about them, you'll also learn a lot about God and his relationship to humanity.

✜ The Bottom Line

There are many good ways to select a passage, and plenty of excellent passages to choose from. Pick an approach that works for you, select your passage, and then move on to step two: observation.

STEP 2
OBSERVATION

What Do I See?

*"Open my eyes that I may see
wonderful things in your law."*
PSALM 119:18

Ask the Spirit of God to be your teacher and to guide you into truth. Ask God for "eyes to see."

As you dive into *Step 2*, remember these four things:

✛ Read, Read, and Read
Don't skim the passage the way you'd click and scroll through the internet looking for something to catch your eye. Study the scene like a detective.

- What do you see? Noticing details requires conscious effort.
- Read the passage a second and third time.
- Don't read things *into* the text, but do try to draw out every relevant detail *from* the text.

✤ Ask Questions

Never be afraid to ask questions. Write down any questions you have about the Bible passage.

✤ Write It Down

Record all your observations. Don't lose those "Aha!" insights by trusting them solely to your memory.

✤ Make Use of Tools

Study Bibles, commentaries, concordances, Bible dictionaries, Bible encyclopedias, interlinear Bibles (Greek and Hebrew to English), Bible handbooks, Bible atlases, time lines, and topical Bibles can all enhance your observations.

Here is a list of questions to help you get started exploring a Bible passage.

OBSERVE THE TEXT

- What are the repeated words, expressions, and ideas in the passage?

- What is the literary genre (form), such as narrative (story), epic, priestly writings, law, liturgy, poetry, lament, teaching, prophecy, gospel, parable, epistle (letter), or apocalyptic literature?

- Are there any synonyms—words that have similar meanings?

- Are there any antonyms—words that have opposite meanings?

- Are there any metaphors, figures of speech, parallelism between lines (such as in poetry), or a specific structure or outline of the passage?

OBSERVE THE CONTEXT

- What comes immediately before and after the Bible passage?

- What is the broader context of the passage? For example, which part of the Old or New Testament is the passage located in? Which book or section of a book is it in?

- Is it a short Bible story within a larger story? Or possibly a specific teaching within a lengthier, more general teaching passage?

OBSERVE THE DETAILS

Ask "Who, What, Where, When, Why, and How?"
Often this information is in the first chapter or in the
introduction to the book. You can also use Bible tools—
such as maps, time lines, and study Bibles—to help you
find answers to the following questions.

Who?

- Who is mentioned or involved here?
- Who seems to be the primary character?
- Who is the original audience?

What?

- What is going on or being said?
- What is the sequence of events?
- What words (verbs, adjectives, prepositions, etc.)
  did the Spirit-guided author choose?
- What descriptive details do I see?
- What is the mood and setting?

Where?

- Where are the events happening?
- Where is the original audience when first hearing
  this passage?

When?

- When is this action taking place?
- What time spans are mentioned?
- Are there any time gaps?

Why?

- Does the author explain why these events are unfolding?
- Does the author offer a motive for a character's words or actions?
- Does the author tell why he is writing this?

How?

- How do the characters respond?
- How does the scene conclude?

Once you've asked all your observation questions, written down your answers, and consulted your tools, it's time to move on to step three: interpretation.

INTERPRETATION

What Does It Mean?

"Cause me to understand the way of your precepts, that I may meditate on your wonderful deeds."
PSALM 119:27

The first thing to keep in mind is this: When interpreting a passage, we are asking, "What does God intend to communicate here?" We are not asking, "What do I feel this passage means to me?" Discerning God's intent may sound like a tall order, but here are some interpretation suggestions to get you started.

✣ Questions to Ask

- What might the original audience have understood the Bible passage to mean?

  For example, in Jesus' parable of the Rich Fool (Luke 12:16–21), what did it mean in Jesus' day for someone to own large barns?

- How do the paragraphs, phrases, or words fit into the author's reason for writing?

  For example, the Gospel writers—Matthew, Mark, Luke, and John—weren't just recording historical events; they wanted show readers that Jesus Christ is the Son of God, the Messiah, and Savior. How might a specific story in their writings fit into the larger message they want to convey about Jesus?

■ How might the type of literature (narrative, poetry, parable, etc.) help us better understand the meaning of the passage?

For example, the New Testament epistles (letters) were written to address specific concerns that early churches faced. When reading the epistles, keep in mind that there is often a backstory—something that has already happened—that can help you better understand the reasons for the specific teachings.

✢ Word Problems

If there is a particular word or phrase in the Bible passage that's confusing, try one or all of these options:

■ Look up the word in a concordance and find other places in Scripture where it's used.

■ Check the notes (usually at the bottom of a page) and the cross-references in a study Bible.

■ Consult a Bible commentary or concordance that shows the words in Greek or Hebrew and gives various meanings for the words.

■ Compare this passage with other Bible translations. Use Bible websites or apps that allow you to look up a passage in multiple translations side by side. This allows you to see how other Bible scholars translated the word or phrase and gives you insight into the nuances of the words.

✢ General Biblical Truths

This is the stage where inductive Bible study moves from the *specific* to the *general*; from the specifics of a Bible passage (or passages) to general biblical truths about God and humanity.

■ What does this Bible passage reveal about who God is and what he is like?

■ What does this passage tell us about human nature?

■ What does this passage explain about the world we live in?

■ Does this passage have anything to say about good or evil?

■ Does this passage teach truths about sin, forgiveness, or salvation?

■ Does this passage teach things about the church or what it means to be a follower of Jesus?

Here are some examples of general biblical truths from Psalm 23—truths about God, human nature, the world, and following Jesus—to help illustrate the interpretation process.

PSALM 23	BIBLICAL TRUTH
The LORD is my shepherd,	Christians are like sheep under Jesus' care. We belong to him.
I lack nothing.	God will meet our deepest needs.
He makes me lie down in green pastures,	God makes us free to rest.
He leads me beside quiet waters,	Shepherds bring their sheep to quiet water to drink. Similarly, God leads us to drink deeply of his Holy Spirit, who is water to our souls.
He refreshes my soul.	God cares for and keeps our hearts and minds.
He guides me along the right paths for his name's sake.	God will lead us on the right path because of his great promise.
Even though I walk through the darkest valley, I will fear no evil, for you are with me;	The world can be frightening, but we don't need to be afraid, because God is with us.
Your rod and your staff, they comfort me.	God's discipline and guidance make us feel safe.
You prepare a table before me in the presence of my enemies.	God provides for us even when we are surrounded by (literal or figurative) enemies.
You anoint my head with oil;	God takes care of our bodily needs,
My cup overflows.	And his provision is abundant.
Surely your goodness and love will follow me all the days of my life,	God's goodness and love will be with us for our whole lives,
And I will dwell in the house of the LORD forever.	And we will live eternally with him.

LIFE APPLICATION

How Does It Apply?

*"I will hasten and not delay
to obey your commands."*

PSALM 119:60

Applying the Bible is the final, crucial step of Bible study. This is where we put God's truth into practice. We live it out. We seek to be doers of the Word (James 1:22). Though a single verse or passage never has multiple interpretations (meanings), it can and does have a myriad of different possible applications. Pray for God's strength to help you grow through your study.

✤ How to Find Good Applications

After you have carefully observed a Bible passage and prayerfully determined what truth God meant to convey through it, you need to state that truth in the form of a broad "now" principle. This serves as a kind of "bridge" between interpretation and application. Here are some questions to help you build that bridge.

✢ The Contemporary Questions

- How can Christians apply what the biblical author has said to the assumptions, values, and goals of our lives and society today?

- What are the general biblical truths found in this passage that apply to our contemporary situation?

- Is there anything this passage has to say about certain social issues, such as racism, justice, poverty, or money?

- How do these verses or principles apply to the church as a body?

✢ The Personal Questions

- What does this Bible passage teach me about . . .
  - › Who I am and how God sees me?
  - › The things I'm worried about and need in my life?
  - › My role in my family, workplace, school, neighborhood, with my friends, and in my local church?
  - › The difficult decisions I face?
  - › My choices regarding sin, forgiveness, and love?
  - › My personal goals and ambitions?
  - › How I talk to and treat others around me?

✛ The Action Questions

- What am I going to do about what I have learned?
- What personal goals am I going to set in my life to implement the truths found in this passage?
- If I act on what I learned from this passage, how might it impact my relationship with God?
- As a result of what I've learned from God's Word, what should I pray about?

For example, a men's group studying Ephesians 5:25 and the command to "love your wives, just as Christ loved the church" all agreed that the timeless principle there is that husbands are called to love their wives unconditionally and sacrificially. But their individual applications of that principle will look very different. For example,

- Bob has decided to back out of his fishing trip, and stay home to do three "honey do" projects that his wife Elizabeth, has been begging him to do for months.
- Stephen feels nudged to apologize to his wife, Ellen, for being a slob and not helping around the house. He wants to give her a weekend at a nice hotel.

This chart shows the differences between the four phases of inductive Bible study.

SELECTION	OBSERVATION	INTERPRETATION	APPLICATION
"I delight in your decrees; I will not neglect your word" (Psalm 119:16).	"Open my eyes that I may see wonderful things from your law" (Psalm 119:18).	"Cause me to understand the way of your precepts, that I may meditate on your wonderful deeds" (Psalm 119:27).	"I will hasten and not delay to obey your commands" (Psalm 119:60).
Asking: What do I study?	Asking: What do I see?	Asking: What does it mean?	Asking: How does it apply?
Planning	Probing	Pondering	Practicing
Engaging	Exploring	Explaining	Exercising
Deciding	Discovering	Digesting	Doing
Starting	Seeing	Understanding	Obeying

THE BIBLE STUDY TOOLBOX

Dictionaries, Maps, Time Lines, Commentaries, and More!

—

TECHNICALLY, ALL you need to do a Bible study is a Bible, prayer, and some time. However, it can be really helpful to have some other tools at your disposal, especially if you're a beginner. This chapter is all about building your Bible study toolbox.

Study Bibles

Study Bibles have introductions, outlines, cross-references, and study notes.

- The **introductions** to each Bible book can give you a ton of background information, answering some of the observation questions about timing, location, and context that might be hard to puzzle out on your own.

- Introduction sections also include **outlines**, which give you a framework to understand the main events in each book. If you're studying a short passage, the outline can help you put it in context.

- **Cross-references** are lists of verses that relate to the passage you're studying. They allow you to quickly see the connections between your passage and the rest of the Bible.

- **Study notes** help explain historical context, difficult concepts, and fascinating facts about Bible passages. If you're studying a tricky passage, the notes are the first place to look for help.

A good study Bible should also have a concordance, maps, and a topical index.

Examples of study Bibles:

- *ESV Study Bible* (Crossway Books & Bibles)
- *NIV Life Application Study Bible* (Zondervan)
- *NKJV Study Bible* (Nelson)
- *The Complete Jewish Study Bible* (Hendrickson)

Concordances

With a concordance, you can look up any word in the Bible. Concordances give an alphabetical listing of:

- key words
- names
- topics

They also include a list of verses that contain each word. This is the tool to use if you want to do a word study or learn about a particular biblical person. Many study Bibles include concordances, but concordances can also be books of their own.

Examples of concordances:

- *Strong's Exhaustive Concordance of the Bible* (Hendrickson)
- *NAS Exhaustive Concordance* (Broadman & Holman)
- *NIV Exhaustive Concordance* (Zondervan)

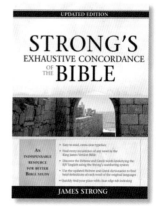

Bible Software and Websites

Bible concordances, dictionaries, translation comparisons, and other resources are often available online. If you'd rather not study with a bunch of big books, Bible software and websites are a great option.

Examples of Bible software and websites:

- Bible Gateway www.biblegateway.com
- Bible Hub www.biblehub.com
- The Unbound Bible www.theunboundbible.com
- The Blue Letter Bible www.blueletterbible.com
- Logos Bible Software www.logos.com

Bible Dictionaries

Like a concordance, a Bible dictionary contains an alphabetical list of terms, names, and topics. But instead of verse references, Bible dictionaries have definitions. Look up words you don't understand, such as *grace*, *redemption*, or *faith.* Expository dictionaries give you more detailed meanings and explanations.

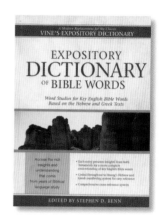

Examples of Bible Dictionaries:

- *Holman Bible Dictionary* (Broadman & Holman)

- *New Illustrated Bible Dictionary* (Nelson)

- *Expository Dictionary of Bible Words* (Hendrickson)

- *New Unger's Dictionary* (Moody)

- *Zondervan's Pictorial Bible Dictionary* (Zondervan)

Bible Atlases, Maps, and Time Lines

These resources are particularly great for visual learners. Atlases, maps, and time lines can help you:

- Learn where Bible events took place.
- Follow along with Bible characters' journeys.
- Compare the locations of ancient cities with their present-day counterparts.
- Understand how biblical events unfolded over thousands of years.
- Put different Bible books (and their authors) in the context of Israel's history.

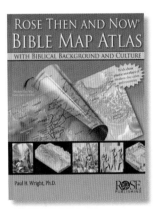

Examples:

- *Rose Then & Now Bible Map Atlas with Biblical Background and Culture* (Rose Publishing)
- *Atlas of Bible Lands* (Broadman & Holman)
- *The New Moody Atlas of the Bible* (Moody)
- *Deluxe Then & Now Bible Maps* (Rose Publishing)
- *Bible Time Line* (Rose Publishing)

Bible Commentaries and Handbooks

Bible commentaries and handbooks, which contain scholars' explanations of Bible books or passages, are incredibly helpful. However, it's a good idea to study the Bible yourself before you turn to a commentary or handbook. You should:

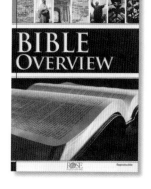

- Study your passage.
- See what it means and how it applies to you.
- List questions you have.
- Look in a commentary to see how scholars have treated your passage.

Examples of Bible commentaries:

- *Matthew Henry's Commentary on the Whole Bible* (Hendrickson Publishers)
- *Eerdmans Commentary on the Bible* (Eerdmans)
- *Bible Knowledge Commentary* (Nelson)

Examples of Bible handbooks:

- *Bible Overview* (Rose Publishing)
- *Holman Bible Handbook* (Broadman & Holman)
- *Halley's Bible Handbook* (Zondervan)

Specialty Bibles

In addition to all the other useful tools, there are specialty Bibles designed to meet your specific needs:

- Topical Bibles organize Scripture into special areas of interest, such as *salvation*, *marriage*, or *prayer*.
- Interlinear Bibles compare the original language (Hebrew or Greek) to modern language.
- Large-print Bibles are easy to read and helpful for many people.
- Bibles specifically for one gender or age group can help people find life applications that fit their situation.

Examples of specialty Bibles:

- *Nave's Topical Bible* (Hendrickson)
- *Topical Analysis of the Bible* (Baker Book House)
- *NLT Everyday Matters Bible for Women* (Hendrickson)
- *KJV Super Giant Print Reference Bible* (Hendrickson)
- *The Interlinear Hebrew-Greek-English Bible* (Hendrickson)

Building a Bible Reference Library

All of these tools can be part of your personal Bible reference library. Check off each category as your library grows.

❏ Study Bible
❏ Concordance
❏ Bible Software and Websites
❏ Bible Dictionary
❏ Bible Atlas and Maps
❏ Bible Time Line
❏ Bible Commentary
❏ Bible Handbook
❏ Specialty Bible

HOW TO TACKLE
THE TOUGH PARTS

—

NOW THAT we've explained how to begin, the four
steps of inductive Bible study, and all the tools in the
Bible study toolbox, let's talk through some of the
tough parts.

Any student of the Bible will tell you that the Bible can
be quite challenging to understand, and sometimes
leave you scratching your head wondering what it
means. But don't give up! God's Word is worth it. Know
this: You will learn more and remember more if you
discover what the Scriptures say yourself.

If you're facing a tough passage of Scripture (and even
when you're not), pray for wisdom and understanding.
Remember what James says: "If any of you lacks
wisdom, you should ask God, who gives generously to
all without finding fault, and it will be given to you"
(James 1:5).

The Five "Do Nots" of Interpretation

1 **Do not** "proof text" (take verses out of context).

- Read the surrounding chapters and the verses before and after the verse you are studying. Get the whole picture. Don't study verses out of context. Look at the outline of the book.

- Take the whole Bible as God's Word. Don't just concentrate on one verse or one idea. See if the teaching is explained more fully in other parts of the Bible.

- Look at the small cross-references in your Bible to help you find other verses on the same subject.

2 **Do not** be too literal.

- Learn to recognize figurative language. (See next section.)

3 **Do not** ignore the Bible's cultural, historical, and literary background.

- Though it's one timeless story, God's Word is comprised of various kinds of literature.

- It was compiled over hundreds of years in a variety of cultural settings by some 40 different human authors writing in three languages—Hebrew, Aramaic, and Greek.

- If we insist on reading it through twenty-first century Western eyes, we will misunderstand its meaning.

4 **Do not** read your own ideas into the Scriptures.

- Be careful not to jump to conclusions. Read the passage several times. Let it sink in.

- We must beware of trying to force a passage to fit with our preexisting beliefs or experiences.

- Disciples should always base their beliefs on what the Bible says rather than interpreting the Bible in accordance with their beliefs.

5 **Do not** get overly creative.

- It's tempting to look for some mysterious, hidden, symbolic meaning that no one has ever seen before. But it's also dangerous.

✥ Instead, you should . . .

Ask and answer a LOT of questions!	For example: ■ What kind of literature is this? Poetry? History? Prophecy? Wisdom? Epistolary? ■ Is this passage narrative (a story) or didactic (instruction)? ■ Is this text descriptive (simply telling about things that happened in a unique setting) or prescriptive (showing what should happen in all places at all times)?
Use the whole of Scripture to help interpret the parts of Scripture.	If other passages do not corroborate your interpretation of a text, you may be on dangerous ground. We should always use clear passages to help us grasp the meanings of unclear ones.
Consider the context of a statement or passage.	For example, to understand Jesus' command to the healed man, "Don't go into the village," in Mark 8, we need to look at comparable passages in Mark's gospel (1:44; 5:19, 43; see also Matthew 8:4 and 16:20).
Consult trustworthy commentaries on Scripture.	Seeing how Bible scholars interpret a text is a valuable help in understanding God's Word. So make use of Bible commentaries and study Bibles with notes from scholars.

Understanding Figurative Language

Figures of speech are word pictures that help us understand a truth. Familiarize yourself with the types of figurative language in the Bible:

✛ Metaphor

"Your word is a lamp for my feet, a light on my path" (Psalm 119:105) is a metaphor that helps us picture the Bible enlightening our minds and actions and giving us direction.

✛ Simile

"As the deer pants for streams of water, so my soul pants for you, my God" (Psalm 42:1) is a simile, which compares ideas with the words "like" or "as." Similes occur over 175 times in the Psalms.

✛ Personification

Jesus used personification when he said if the people did not declare the mighty works they had seen God do, the stones would cry out in praise (Luke 19:40).

✛ Hyperbole (Exaggeration)

Hyperbole is found in Matthew 5:29–30:

> "If your right eye causes you to stumble, gouge it out and throw it away. It is better for you to lose one part of your body than for your whole body to be thrown into hell. And if your right hand causes you to stumble, cut it off and throw it away. It is better for you to lose one part of your body than for your whole body to go into hell."

Discovering the Intended Meaning

As you read the Bible, look for the author's intended meaning.

- What did the author want to say?
- What did it mean in that culture?
- What did it mean to the original audience?
- What are the main ideas the author is pointing out?

If you have questions, write them down, pray for insight, and discuss your ideas with others.

Knowing the Author's Intent

Imagine a terminally ill billionaire has drawn up her last will and testament. After her funeral, when the will is read by a probate court, what's the goal? Is it to discover and do what she actually intended, or is it to have family factions interpret her words in five very different ways and bicker over the matter for the next twenty years? Obviously the goal of a good attorney and a non-biased judge is to disregard what all the readers of the will want it to mean, and to discern and carry out the intent of the author of the will. And so it is with interpreting God's Word. His intent must be our goal.

BIBLE BACKGROUND

———

WE'VE ALREADY covered what you need to know about the Bible, but here is some more historical background and in-depth advice that will prepare you to tackle both the Old and New Testaments.

Reading the Old Testament

The Old Testament can be intimidating. However, making the effort to read and understand the Old Testament produces great fruit in our lives. In the many stories, poems, prophecies, songs, prayers, pieces of wisdom, and instructions of the Old Testament, we see the way God relates to humanity, both his people in particular and the nations in general.

Here are some things to keep in mind when reading the Old Testament:

✢ The Old Testament is as much the Word of God as the New Testament.

Though the Old Testament was compiled over hundreds of years and written by many different authors, it all originated with God. It is his Word to his people.

The apostle Peter reminds believers, "We also have the prophetic message as something completely reliable.... No prophecy of Scripture came about by the prophet's own interpretation of things. For prophecy never had its origin in the human will, but prophets, though human, spoke from God as they were carried along by the Holy Spirit" (2 Peter 1:19–21).

✦ The Old Testament helps us understand the New Testament.

The Old Testament deals with events and teachings hundreds—and even thousands—of years before Jesus was born. Those events and teachings give us the background to all that happened when Jesus was born and during his life. For example, understanding the Old Testament sacrifices sheds light on what Jesus' sacrifice on the cross means. Knowing about the

Old Testament prophecies of a coming Messiah helps us see how Jesus is that Messiah (the "Christ") who fulfills God's promises given long ago. The Old Testament laws, customs, and religious traditions help us make sense of Jesus' interactions with the Jewish religious leaders of his day.

✢ God's grace for humanity is seen throughout the Old Testament.

As we read the Old Testament, we begin to understand the gracious and powerful God who created all things. We also understand the need for God's grace as we contemplate human folly and sin. Because of his grace, rather than destroying humanity, God planned to save us.

We see this plan unfold in the pages of the Old Testament. It is not always a straightforward telling of God's plan. Often, we must carefully find God's plan in the stories of people who, just like us today, experienced the goodness of creation, the corruption of a good creation, the terrible distorting power of sin, and the sad consequences of separation from God.

✢ Old Testament people and stories serve as examples for believers today.

The apostle Paul tells us that the things that happened to people in the Old Testament "happened to them as examples and were written down as warnings for us, on whom the culmination of the ages has come. So, if you think you are standing firm, be careful that you don't fall!" (1 Corinthians 10:11–12).

Even the most faithful people in the Old Testament, like Moses and King David, fell into sin and were disciplined by God. Yet, in the Old Testament we see how God continued to redeem and restore his people even after terrible sin and tragedy.

✤ The Old Testament helps us recognize God's actions.

Although we are not of the world, Jesus has sent us to the world to be witnesses of his love, grace, and sacrifice. As long as we are, we must learn to recognize the way God moves and acts in the world, both through people and in extraordinary ways that do not require people. The more we read the Old Testament, the more we learn to recognize God's ways in the world.

Reading the New Testament

The events in the New Testament take place in a time of political difficulties. The Roman Empire had tightened its fist around regions like Judea, where people were unwilling to bow down to the Roman emperors. Many Jews hoped and prayed for a liberating Messiah to come, drive the Romans away from Jerusalem, and rebuild the kingdom of David.

The Sermon of the Beatitudes
by James Tissot

God did send the Messiah, but he was not the Messiah they were expecting. He is much more than a political leader: he is the Savior who conquered death, defeated evil and sin, allows us a direct relationship with God, and offers eternal life.

✤ Four Gospels, One Jesus

The term gospel was used in the Roman world as an imperial proclamation, the good news of the deeds of the Caesar. However, in the New Testament, the good news these books present is about "Jesus the Messiah, the Son of God" (Mark 1:1).

The Gospels tell a story about the actions and teachings of Jesus. In his life and words, Jesus proclaimed the coming of God's kingdom. God's promises to his people in the Old Testament are now fulfilled in Jesus.

The Raising of Lazarus
by Duccio di Buoninsegna

However, we do not find just one story about Jesus. Rather we find four similar yet distinctive stories. Matthew, Mark, Luke, and John tell us about Jesus' life and work from four related perspectives. Why are there four Gospels instead of just one? One answer is that it takes four points of view to get the whole story about Jesus. Some might argue that one authoritative story should be enough. However, God chose to reveal himself using four Gospels.

Transfiguration of Christ
by Carl Bloch

The Gospel of John begins with these words: "In the beginning was the Word.... The Word became flesh" (1:1, 14). God chooses to speak to humans by means of other humans. This is true of the Bible and it is supremely true of Christ, whom we are told is God in the flesh (John 1:14–18). So then, the Gospels are, like Jesus, both a Divine work and a human work. They have real human authors and one divine Author. They give details that might be difficult to understand, but they are never truly contradictory. They have four different points of view on the history of Jesus, but only one Divine conclusion as to his identity as the Son of God.

GOSPEL	AUDIENCE	JESUS THE SON OF GOD
Matthew	Jewish world	Is the Messiah King of Israel
Mark	Greek-speaking world	Is the Power of God in the world
Luke	Gentile world	Is the Ideal Man of God
John	Whole world	Is the Word of God

Christ Rescuing Peter from Drowning by Lorenzo Veneziano

✤ The First Christians and Their Writings

THE BOOK OF ACTS

The book of Acts is a natural continuation of the Gospels. The good news of Jesus continues in the work of Jesus' disciples in Jerusalem and throughout the world. In the book of Acts we find God's plan for humanity being played out in the life of the early Christians, who embodied Jesus' ministry and announced the good news of salvation to all peoples.

Similar to the Historical Books in the Old Testament, the book of Acts gives identity to God's people today by showing us how God's mission spread to all people and nations of the world.

Although the apostles Peter and Paul play a significant role in the book, the main characters of the book are God and the church. Paul and Peter lay the foundations for the spread of the gospel and illustrate the ministry of the Holy Spirit through the apostles. Acts tells about the spread of the gospel. For that reason, it's good to have some knowledge of the places Christians visited and of the cultures in those places to better understand the importance of the book.

The Four Purposes of the Book of Acts

- **Proclamation:** The book of Acts proclaims the good news of Jesus Christ. It presents the gospel message.

- **Apologetic:** It defends Christianity as a source of blessing.

- **Unifying:** It shows the importance of preaching the gospel to Jew and Gentile alike.

- **Teaching:** It's a book of instruction for believers. The history of the book of Acts is the history of God's people.

THE LETTERS

The letters (or epistles) make up twenty-one of the twenty-seven books in the New Testament. They contain vital information for Christians and their journey through life. Whereas the Gospels present the good news of Jesus—his life and ministry—the epistles explain the effects of Jesus' ministry, the coming of the Holy Spirit, and the spread of the gospel through Jerusalem, Judea, Samaria, and the Gentile world.

There are different kinds of epistles in New Testament:

- Personal letters, such as Philemon, which is written to a specific individual.
- Circular letters, such as Ephesians, which was a letter meant to be circulated among several churches in a region.
- Letters to a specific congregation, such as 1 and 2 Corinthians, which were written to the church congregation in the city of Corinth.
- Other letters do not name the author or the recipients, such as Hebrews, which does

not name its author, and 1 John, which does not indicate its recipient. Others look only in a very general way like a letter at all (James).

However, all the letters share some important features. The first, and most important, is that they are divine communications for God's people in the early church and throughout history.

Another important consideration about these New Testament letters is that they are occasional documents. This means that each letter was written to address a specific set of issues, at a specific time, and in a specific place. This point is important to keep in mind because it highlights the value in knowing as much about the context of the letter as possible. It also reminds us that none of the letters, or even all of them put together, represents the full theology of Paul, Peter, or John. Rather, they were addressing specific issues. Those issues determined the content of each letter.

However, understanding the issues that each letter addresses is not easy. Often, reading the letters can feel like listening in on a person's phone conversation; we know only half of it.

THE BOOK OF REVELATION

The book of Revelation is not an epistle; rather, it belongs to a special category or genre of writing known as apocalyptic literature. *Apocalyptic* is a type of literature that reveals God's previously hidden plans to humanity.

Interpreting Revelation has always been a great challenge for Christians. However, its message is much too important to simply ignore. We must approach the book with a sense of respect and wonder, but also with the confidence that God's message in the book is still relevant.

Despite the many disagreements about the meaning of Revelation, there are important agreements among Christians:

- The message of the book is relevant for Christians today, as it was for Christians in the times of the apostles.

- The main purpose of the book is to provide hope and encouragement for believers at all times, especially in times of persecution or suffering.
- The message of the book is clear on at least three points:
  - Christ is coming back and will judge humanity;
  - the powers of evil are doomed before Christ; and
  - God promises a wonderful future for all who believe in Christ.

LET'S TRY IT!
A SAMPLE BIBLE STUDY

LET'S LOOK at the components of inductive Bible study in more detail by doing a simple Bible study together.

STEP 1: Selection

This time, we've done *Step 1* for you, and selected Mark 8:22–26. Here's the passage:

> They came to Bethsaida, and some people brought a blind man and begged Jesus to touch him. He took the blind man by the hand and led him outside the village. When he had spit on the man's eyes and put his hands on him, Jesus asked, "Do you see anything?"
>
> He looked up and said, "I see people; they look like trees walking around."
>
> Once more Jesus put his hands on the man's eyes. Then his eyes were opened, his sight was restored, and he saw everything clearly. Jesus sent him home, saying, "Don't even go into the village."

STEP 2: Observation

Remember, you have four things to do:

1 Read Mark 8:22–26 multiple times, drawing out all the relevant details from the text.

- Read the verses immediately before and after the passage too, so that you can see the story in context.

2 Ask questions. What more do you want to know about the passage?

- In addition to asking specific questions that occurred to you while you were reading, you can refer back to the list of questions suggested earlier in this book under *Step 2: Observation.*

3 Write your questions and observations down, so you don't lose track of your insights.

- Make a list of who the characters are, what they're doing, where and when the story is taking place, and why and how the events are unfolding.
- Note repeated words, concepts, and actions.

4 Use the tools in your toolbox. See if a study Bible, commentary, concordance, Bible dictionary, atlas, time line, etc. can answer your questions or supplement your observations. In this case, we have a few suggestions:

- Refer to a map to find out where Bethsaida is.

- Use cross-references to find out if there are any similar stories elsewhere in the Bible.

- Use a time line of Jesus' life or ministry to see where this story fits in.

- Look in a commentary or study Bible to learn more about

  › What it was like to be blind in biblical times,

  › Why Jesus used spit to heal someone,

  › Whether there's anything unusual about this healing, and

  › Any other questions you have.

STEP 3: Interpretation

Once you've done the hard work of gathering facts—
objectively asking, "What do I see?"—it's time to begin
asking, "What does all this mean?"

It's helpful to approach this question as a transition
from the specific details of the passage to the broader
truths and timeless principle it conveys.

You might ask the following:

- What does this passage communicate about
  › Jesus' character?
  › Jesus' interactions with people in need?
  › Human nature?
  › What it means to be a follower of Jesus?

Your answers to these questions can help lead you
toward application.

STEP 4: **Life Application**

Applications are the most individualized part of Bible study. Once you've settled on what the passage communicates (interpretation), you can start thinking about how it applies to your contemporary culture and personal situation.

For example, in the case of our passage, Mark 8:22–26, it might be good to ask:

- Does this passage affect how I view or treat people with disabilities?
- Are there areas in my life that require Jesus' compassion and healing?
- Are there any changes I should implement in my life on the basis of this passage?
- How would acting on what I've learned from this passage affect my relationship with God?
- How should I pray in response to this passage?

Some Bible passages will have more direct, actionable applications than others, depending both on the passage and on your situation in life. Don't feel pressure to come out of every Bible study with concrete action items. However, do allow each Bible study to expand your knowledge of God and enrich your relationship with him.

THE GOAL OF BIBLE STUDY

THE GOAL of Bible study is a transformed life and a deep relationship with God. When you listen and respond to what God is telling you through his Word, you will be amazed at the results in your life as your relationship with him deepens. Let yourself be amazed by what God will show you in and through his Word!

As you study Scripture, you will often see a command to obey, an example to follow, a lesson to learn, or a sin to confess. Apply that to your life.	"Do not merely listen to the word, and so deceive yourselves. Do what it says" (James 1:22).
Sometimes, you will want to claim a promise, pray a prayer, forgive someone, or ask forgiveness. Listen to the "still small voice" of God.	"Be still and know that I am God" (Psalm 46:10).
Other times, you'll simply be amazed at what God is saying and doing. You'll want to fall to your knees in worship, jump up and shout for joy, or lift your hands and sing praises to your heavenly Father!	When crowds witnessed Jesus miraculously healing people, they "were amazed . . . and they praised the God of Israel" (Matthew 15:30–31).

Seven Reasons to Study the Bible

❶ To Know God

Bible study is not only for knowing *about* God, it's for *knowing* God himself.

❷ To Love God

The more we know God, the more we can love him. The Great Commandment is to love God with all of our being and our neighbor as ourselves: "The most important one…is this: 'Hear, O Israel: The Lord our God, the Lord is one. Love the Lord your God with all your heart and with all your soul and with all your mind and with all your strength.' The second is this: 'Love your neighbor as yourself.' There is no commandment greater than these" (Mark 12:29–31). Meditate on God's character, principles, and promises. Rejoice in his love, care, and forgiveness.

❸ To Learn Truth

The Scriptures were inspired by God. They teach us the truth and show us what is wrong in our lives. They straighten us out. As the apostle Paul explains, "All Scripture is God-breathed [inspired] and is useful for teaching, rebuking, correcting and training in righteousness, so that the servant of God may be thoroughly equipped for every good work" (2 Timothy 3:16–17).

④ To Discover Direction in Life

The Bible shows us what to do. Studying God's Word can help you see your next step: "Your word is a lamp for my feet, a light on my path" (Psalm 119:105).

⑤ To Find Comfort and Hope

God's Word give us encouragement. Many people in the Bible faced times of trial and severe suffering. You can find hope by learning from their stories—by listening to the words God spoke to them when they were at their lowest points. In Isaiah, God says to his people, "Do not fear, for I am with you; do not be dismayed, for I am your God. I will strengthen you and help you; I will uphold you with my righteous right hand" (41:10).

⑥ To Repent of Sin

The Bible helps us see ourselves as we really are and convicts us of sin so that we repent and change. Let God's Word expose your innermost thoughts and desires, as Hebrews 4:12–15 tells us: "The word of God is alive and active. Sharper than any double-edged sword, it penetrates even to dividing soul and spirit, joints and marrow; it judges the thoughts and attitudes of the heart. Nothing in all creation is hidden from God's sight. Everything is uncovered and laid bare before the eyes of him to whom we must give account."

7 To Be Sanctified

Jesus prayed for his followers that they would be sanctified: "Sanctify them by the truth; your word is truth" (John 17:17). To be sanctified means to be made holy, to be set apart by God for a special purpose. God has a plan and purpose for our lives. Immersing ourselves in God's Word helps us become the kind of people God wants us to be.

> *"Apply yourself to the whole text, and apply the whole text to yourself."*
>
> —JOHANN ALBRECHT BENGEL

MADE EASY

by Rose Publishing

The *Made Easy* series helps you quickly find biblical answers to important questions. These pocket-sized books are packed with clear explanations and key facts you need to know.

THE BOOKS OF THE BIBLE MADE EASY
Quick summaries of all 66 books of the Bible
ISBN 9781628623420

BIBLE STUDY MADE EASY
A step-by-step guide to studying God's Word
ISBN 9781628623437

WORLD RELIGIONS MADE EASY
30 religions and how they compare to Christianity
ISBN 9781628623451

UNDERSTANDING THE HOLY SPIRIT MADE EASY
Who the Holy Spirit is and what he does
ISBN 9781628623444

www.hendricksonrose.com